Far From Crazy –

Success In Sanity:

My Unashamed Truth

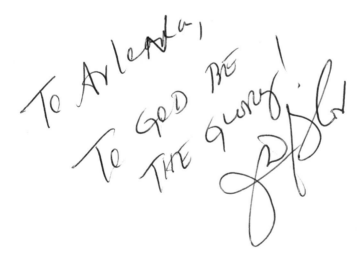

Jessica Johnson Glover

Far From Crazy – Success In Sanity: My Unashamed Truth

Copyright © 2022 by Jessica Johnson Glover

ISBN (978-1-7375310-8-1)

Disclaimer: The following versions of the Bible may have been referenced: New International Version (NIV), King James Version (KJV), New Living Translation (NLT), English Standard Version (ESV), New King James (NKJV), New International Reader's Version (NIRV), Christian Standard Bible (CSB), Common English Bible (CEB), The Message (MSG).

MTE Publishing
mtepublishing.com

Table of Contents

Dedication

This book is dedicated to everyone who has struggled with understanding and accepting the realities of mental illness.

Special Thanks & Acknowledgements

To my father, the late Mr. Jesse Johnson, your love for me remains in my soul. Little reminders of you are a constant in my life. You battled this storm before me. Your challenges provided answers to mine. I will forever be your namesake, daddy's first baby girl.

To my mother, the queen, Mrs. Dianna Grant Johnson, THANK YOU for your undying and unconditional love. You have held my hand through every season of my life. For that, I am forever grateful. Your sacrifice to ensure that we all become the highest version of ourselves is priceless. I am proud to be your #1 diamond!

To my *guardfather*, the late Mr. Alvin "Buster" Mitchell, the lessons you taught me about life and the importance of manifesting my dreams are invaluable. Thank you for stirring up the gifts in me and requiring me to be myself no matter what anyone has to say about it!

To my *guardmother*, Mrs. Helen Mitchell, THANK YOU for supporting my parents in raising me. Your love and reminder that "All Things Considered, I AM GOOD" will remain with me forever. I love you to LIFE!

To my king, my husband, Gerald Lamar Glover, THANK YOU for partnering with me in life. Your love is palpable. You speak to my spirit, handle my heart with care, soothe my mind, and empower my soul. I look forward to leaving a lasting legacy and making a mark in this world that will never be erased with you! We are TEAM GLOVER FOREVER!

To Marcos and Jocelyn Johnson Stephens, The Late Javida Johnson Coonce, Reginald Coonce, Jr., and Arin L. Johnson THANK YOU for coming to my aid in every season of my life. As my siblings, each of you have helped me understand the value of family.

To My Village, THANK YOU for walking with me over the last forty-five years. Your love, support, inspiration, and example mean the world to me.

To Jaela Stephens, Morgan Stephens, Bethany Stephens, Zion Johnson-Jennings, Skyla Stephens, Vernon Campbell Stephens, Roger D'jimon Fleming, Arriyanna Fleming, Asia Fleming, Tiffany Gibbons, Ariel Baker and Arina Baker...I love each of you. As my tribe of nieces, nephews, godchildren, and grand godchildren, you represent the vessels God allows me the opportunity to pour into.

I pray this book teaches you something about me, my life, and my mission. If you or anyone you know faces any type of mental health challenge, I want you to know that with God, family support, medication, and therapy, there are solutions.

I never want you to see mental health challenges as a scorned secret. If you aren't feeling like yourself, talk about it. Seek therapy. Seek help. There is nothing to be ashamed of. A healthy mind is vital to your success in life. Go forth in this world and CONQUER every dream you have. Leave this world empty. Complete every assignment given by God in your life!

Foreword

By Gerald Lamar Glover

For better or for worse. The former part of this vow gets a lot of attention, but the latter is often selectively forgotten. Immediately, when our spiritual father said those words to me and Jessica; I intentionally honed in on the gravity of the better (who wants to think about the worst). God's plan included me marrying my very best friend. So, I stood proudly in front of my bride to be, with visions of joy and happiness together. These dreams of mine were not cultivated in childhood but manifested in adulthood and through my relationship with Jesus Christ.

I was content. Although, I did not know all of the answers or where our path would lead us - I trusted God and my wifey! This is where my zoe resides. The seeds of prayer sown from our ancestors on our behalf, even before we were twinkles in our parent's eyes, were showing up as a harvest in a shared love. We selected our scripture and wedding symbol:

Ecclesiastes 4:12 - "Though one may be overpowered, two can defend themselves. A cord of three strands is not quickly broken."

Little did we know, as we intertwined the white, gold, and purple cords together, in front of our family and the world, we also encountered pitfalls, obstacles, dangers, and long-term suffering, that we would not be separated from the promise of full life. We were determined to see and experience the goodness of the Lord. This is what we stood on, and still stand on, today. The Lord sent my mate, and she is strong, resilient, and full of faith.

I met my wife at work. Right off the top, I was taken aback. She was beautiful, intelligent, and funny. Her mind was sharp, and being even playfully disrespectful, would elicit a strong response from her. She is disarmingly kind, but to believe she was vulnerable, weak, or a pushover, would be a mistake. We developed a friendship, and over time, transitioned into a relationship. We bonded over family and faith. As we were raised, we saw our parents married for decades. The foundation of building a family was there. In our dating life, we caught ourselves in the car singing the gospel song, *Sign Me up for the Christian Jubilee*, by Warner Williams and Jay Summerour. We knew all the words, sang as both the chorus, and the deacon who previewed the next line in the song. We knew something special was brewing between us.

Settling into married life, we sifted through the opportunities and desires we had as individuals, and now, as a married couple. Where to live, where to work, paying bills, time with friends and family, and managing our shared life. I enjoyed every bit of it because we had a chance to build together. Life was a blank canvas, and we painted our vision. My wife took medication to counter a chemical imbalance that could impact her behavior. We discussed it on our very first date, and it was never an issue for me. She took her medicine, and I never saw behavior from her that was out of the ordinary. My wife had a desire to have children. In order to make that happen, the drugs that gave her balance could no longer be taken. To make this family addition, we would need to risk my wife's health – and peace.

My wife's behavior started to change, almost instantly. She was irritable, aggressive, and suspicious of everyone around her – including me. My response was patience and understanding. One of the side effects of this illness is the push towards isolation. It was not just her isolating, I began to feel protective of her image, and how others perceived her. I said to myself, "Sure, we will figure this out," but I didn't want anyone thinking my love was less than. She would yell at me and say hurtful things to me, but I refused to budge. I believed faithfully that she would be made whole. But my faith alone could not help my wife completely and I wasn't trained to recognize the signs of mental illness. My wife was declining, and I could not pull her up by myself. I felt sad, inadequate, and frustrated at times. I'm *her* husband. The Provider. The Protector. However, my bravado could not keep her... That could only be done with God, her commitment to sanity and success, and my vow to be her HUSBAND for better or worse.

It was during my wife's recovery from her mental break that I developed the greatest admiration for her. At her highest and lowest points, her faith remained consistent in God. I saw her beat back depression, hopelessness, despair, and anguish. I saw her tackle challenges like new medication, returning to the workforce, and integrating back into society, with vigor and tenacity. At every level of her ascent, she gave God all the glory. Her life was not returning to normal. She was being elevated in an ongoing cavalcade of awards, promotions, and unmerited favor. She prayed for a hill and got placed on a mountaintop. The harvest is real, but the view is miraculously breathtaking!

Blessings are never singular events. God's innate brilliance includes interweaving His will into our lives. Jessica has sown throughout her lifetime in bettering the lives of others. Her uncompromising, giving nature shows up in every conversation she has. If an individual is looking for a job... She unconsciously starts searching sites for who's hiring. If someone needs furniture... She will start shaking her network tree for items. If a person wants to go to college... Please don't try to stop her from researching grants and scholarships! Jessica's compassion for others reflects the love God has granted to her. I now invite you to experience my wife, Jessica Denean Johnson Glover's story. Her life so far exudes survival, and tragedies that transformed into triumphant victories! She is unforgettable and Jessica's message is life changing and life-saving.

Introduction: Secret *In* Sanity

No one wants to be called crazy! It's insulting, condescending, and cruel. Prior to the age of 25, I hadn't questioned my mental health. I never thought my sanity would be something I had to literally fight for! However, my father was admitted into a mental health facility when I was 15-years-old. The topic itself is touchy and I still don't quite understand fully what happened to my father at the onset of his illness.

In the winter of 1993, my mom left a note on the kitchen counter stating that my dad was going to the hospital. He was at a psychiatric hospital for a few weeks. Family members came down and visited him. Daddy was heavily medicated, and the experience was very confusing. My mom held up the best she could and encouraged my sisters and I to see him. She'd gently remind us to tell him we loved him. I could tell mom really struggled with articulating and accepting dad's mental breakdown.

Like most Black women, mom has this indescribable quiet strength. She walked out her faith during their 40-year marriage. When daddy was sick, she took on two jobs to help pay for my college education and covered household expenses—We lacked nothing.

When I graduated high school, I decided to major in psychology because daddy needed help—fast! Nevertheless, dad and I kept an open line of communication... We were very close. In fact, I was named after him! I'm such a daddy's girl. I look like him, talk like him and would do anything for him. I was his mini me.

Sometimes the things daddy shared with me fell under the "TMI" category, and I'd tell him, "You don't have to share that, daddy!" I wish he would have trusted a therapist as much as he trusted me. I know this form of treatment would have been beneficial. We never talked about "it". It was taboo to even verbalize that mental illness was our family's secret reality. Like I stated previously, nobody wants to be called crazy!

Exactly 10 years after the onset of my father's mental health battle, in January 2003, I survived my first mental breakdown. I was confused, lost, and completely unaware of how I would find my way back to sanity.

Chapter 1

Love High

Love brings out the best and worst in us. I fell in love for the first time when I was 12-years-old and he was 14-years-old. Looking at him gave me quivers… even when we were in church; and no, I wasn't feeling the spirit! My teenage emotions were in overdrive; we crushed on each other. I believed our future included hearing, "I now pronounce you husband and wife," one day.

When he graduated high school, he went off to Morehouse College. Two years later, I moved to Atlanta to attend Clark Atlanta University. Somehow our paths continued to cross over the years.

After Christmas break in Jacksonville, I went back to Atlanta. Before arriving back, we set a date and time to see each other. We hadn't seen each other in a few years. I made a beautiful soul food dinner and we laughed and talked for hours. We were inseparable, it was nine days of complete bliss. He was a minister and single; I was single, too. He'd pray with me, and we'd read scriptures together—things seemed to align perfectly.

We both called out of work and explored Atlanta...from apartment scouting and trying new restaurants, to going on bowling dates (in the middle of the day), everything felt so right.

It was almost like we were destined to be because we grew up together and our families knew each other. We literally planned our future. We talked about starting a family and ministry together.

On the 9th day of January, my crush decided that we had to get back to a sense of reality and he returned to work. I was off that day and was still basking in our newly rekindled love. I was so excited that I could not sleep. My mind was racing. I was planning every aspect of our future. From where we would live, what our wedding would entail, how many children we'd have...my mind wouldn't stop, and I stayed up all night.

On the following day, Friday, January 10, 2003, I found myself very tired, so I decided to try to take an afternoon nap. It was a cool day in Atlanta, so I turned the heat up in my apartment, took a shower, put on my pajamas, and got under the covers. I began reading Ephesians 2:19-22 which references Jesus Christ being the Chief Cornerstone. My mind was all over the place. I took the cornerstone reference in the scripture literally. I began placing my bible in the corner of my bed with pillows, like a make-shift altar. I began singing praise songs unto God. I was exhausted but I couldn't rest because my mind was speeding with thoughts about God, my new love, and the future.

It was around noon when I suddenly jumped out of bed. I took off my pajamas, grabbed my black Gucci purse and my African wooden cane and walked out of the front door of my apartment—completely naked!

I remember everything now in slow motion. My mind was moving at lightning speed, I saw another resident look at me in disbelief as I walked across the street to the leasing office in broad daylight. When I opened the door to the office, the leasing manager yelled my name… "JESSICA!", and I immediately felt a huge sense of relief. Finally, someone could help me. I didn't realize my mind snapped. I just knew something wasn't right, and I needed help.

She rushed me into the bathroom of the leasing office. I was in the bathroom still singing praise songs. I began to sing louder because the acoustics made me sound better. The leasing manager went to my apartment, gathered my clothes, called my parents in Jacksonville, and then an ambulance. I got dressed, waited while being totally engrossed with various praise songs until the ambulance arrived.

While riding in the ambulance, one of the EMTs took out a pocket bible, read a few scriptures to me and prayed over me. She told me that I would be OK and to continue to trust in my Lord and Savior Jesus Christ. I was taken to the Kennestone Hospital Emergency Room.

My parents and baby sister rushed to Atlanta. They were there by 7 p.m. that evening. I was still singing songs when they arrived. My mind was still in another place. It was like my mind was floating in its own world, totally disconnected from reality in a very high place. I kept referring to my baby sister as my "wisdom" and my other sister as my "joy". I was applying biblical concepts to my altered sense of reality. Although my mind snapped, I have never felt closer to God and his Word. In my spirit, I knew I would be fine, I just didn't know what was ahead.

My mother, auntie-cousin, and baby sister comforted me in the ER, while my father waited outside. I was then admitted to the psychiatric ward, the same place I visited my father, **10** years earlier.

Chapter 2

No Straight Jacket... Just Coming to Grips

I was still singing even as my vitals were being taken. I remember the nurse telling me that I needed to be quiet because the other patients were sleeping. My intake process took about 45 minutes or so. I was given medication and I went to bed. At that point, I hadn't slept in 48 hours.

Nevertheless, the next morning, I couldn't help but notice countless patients (men and women) walking around like zombies. I sort of understood why I was there, but I didn't know exactly what was going on. The fact that the institution was familiar to me (because daddy had been there), was a weird type of comfort. I majored in psychology but was also curious about my family's history and just how serious of a diagnosis I would receive. We, as a family, never discussed mental illness. Over the years, I heard whisperings about relatives having various experiences and challenges mentally, but no one would ever tell the whole story. Where did this originate? What were the diagnoses? Who else suffered from mental health issues? What types of medications were family members taking? There was shame and embarrassment surrounding the topic.

I was there for about two weeks, but it seemed like two years. The staff's focus for the first week was getting my medication right. So, I spent a lot of time participating in activities. I attended support groups, played games, and socialized with other patients between the three meals each day. Staff wouldn't allow us to stay in bed all day, so they tried to keep us busy.

The second week was full of assessments to help ensure I could re-enter society. The psychiatrists would ask me questions like what day of the week was it, what city was I in and my date of birth. I thought the interrogation was unnecessary in a way because I could answer them in a blink. However, I knew something was off, but I was ready to go. Deep inside, I believed my sanity had returned. However, when I was given medication at night, it made me feel like I was going to shut down. My biggest adjustment was getting used to how the medication made me feel. I also knew that I didn't want to sit at home all day; I wanted to return to work and live a normal lifestyle.

I spent most of my time making friends, ministering to the patients, praying for them, and singing gospel songs. Even in the middle of my mental breakdown, God sent an angel in the form of a nurse.

She was a Black woman, in her mid-forties, with a calming voice. This lady didn't treat me like I was crazy, she treated me like I was on a "real" road to recovery. We would sing, "The Blood Will Never Lose Its Power" by Andrae Crouch, as she gave me my meds every night. She would even tell me when I was off key. I grew up singing that song in church. The lyrics touch me deeply and continue to move me to tears to this day:

The blood that Jesus shed for me

Way back on Calvary

The blood that gives me strength

From day to day

It will never lose its power

It reaches to the highest mountain

It flows to the lowest valley

The blood that gives me strength

From day to day

It will never lose its power

It soothes my doubts and calms my fears

And it dries all my tears

The blood that gives me strength

From day to day

It will never lose its power

It reaches to the highest mountain

It flows to the lowest valley

The blood that gives me strength

From day to day

It will never lose its power

She also gave me holy communion and she prayed over me. Then one day she told me that my medication is a form of healing. Therefore, I accepted this temporary reality because I believed one day I would outgrow "it".

Although I had a real psychotic breakdown, I knew what I wanted. I created a vision board before vision boards were a thing. I ripped out pages from magazines and put pictures of diamond rings, luxury homes and fancy cars that I wanted in a folder.

When my crush came to visit, I shared the folder with him. I told him that these are the things that we could work towards acquiring together once I got out of the hospital. I could tell he was scared out of his mind! Eventually, he stopped answering my calls and never visited me again. That's when I realized our relationship was over.

I was taken back to Jacksonville to live with my parents. I was single, jobless, and indigent. Unsurprisingly, I didn't have a pity party. I have never been one to just bow down and die... I was purposed for more, and I knew it, I also knew I was far from crazy.

Chapter 3

Chasing a Dream That Wasn't My Destiny

After trying to get my footing back in Jacksonville, I was frustrated. I felt like I was a big fish in a small pond. I felt like everyone was watching to see if I could rebound from this event. I know that I was probably creating these ideas, but I truly longed to be back in a place where I could live my life without being under a microscope. So, I went back to Atlanta and stayed with my auntie-cousin until I got on my feet [or so I thought]. A part of me was chasing my crush while the other part of me was chasing my why. I struggled with accepting my diagnosis of bipolar disorder while trying to create some sense of normalcy.

I was in a very dark place and suffered from depression. I learned through my caring auntie-cousin that I also had poor hygiene. Sometimes I would go three days without taking a shower. It was hard to create a daily routine because it was a chore to motivate myself to get out of bed. Not to mention being on time for work while fighting Atlanta rush-hour traffic. Battling depression is a major feat. It literally sucked the life out of me. I was in a constant battle trying to regain my sanity. Outside of work, I stayed inside of the house. I'd devour an entire container of banana pudding ice cream in one sitting while watching movies for hours. I was just coping and drawing in my sanity.

Eventually, my mom called, and we had a heart-to-heart conversation that led me back to Jacksonville. If my mom could have come through the phone, she would have. She was eager to have me back home to keep a close watch on me. I'm sure knowing I had bipolar disorder made her think of daddy's struggles with mental illness as well.

Nevertheless, I was somewhat relieved to be relocating. I knew that starting over was what I needed. So, in 2004, I returned to Jacksonville and started working in the mortgage industry. I couldn't help but think about the pictures of beautiful homes I tore from magazines. I yearned to have a beautiful home, a husband, and children... I wanted a life even better than what I imagined. I was chasing the dream that I longed to be my destiny! This is when I met my husband Gerald L. Glover, affectionately called, "Glover".

Chapter 4

Holding *My Belt* for a Minute

I had this conversation on my first date with Glover. It is now 17 years later.

"Remember during our phone call, last night, I mentioned an illness that I suffer from?"

"Yes, I do."

"I have bipolar disorder; it's a *mental* illness... My father has it also."

"Do you take your medication?"

"Yes, I do."

"Well, good! We'll be fine then."

We never talked about it again, until almost eight years later.

Glover and I met at a local Jacksonville mortgage company about two months after I started. I was sitting at my desk, taking sales calls. I'd just hung up with a customer and he walked over to my desk and said, "Hello, my team had to evacuate from their desks because there was a small fire in the building. I left my lunch. You wouldn't happen to have any snacks?" I replied, "As a matter of fact, I do. Do you want some canned peaches?" He said, "PEACHES!? Who keeps peaches at their desk?" I blushed and said, "I DO!"

That started a playful banter between the two of us. A few months later, I sat next to him at a benefits meeting. We laughed and flirted a bit. He was always so happy and full of life. Every time I saw him, he made me smile.

One day, I was at my desk, and I saw him coming down the hallway, but this time he was looking for me. Once he spotted me, I felt butterflies. His confidence was alluring, and I couldn't help but wonder what he would say. "Hey, how's your day going? I was in the area, so I wanted to check on you."

When he left, my coworker said, "Tomorrow, you need to go visit him at his desk!" I did JUST THAT! I made sure I was cute, too! My lipstick was fresh. My hair was curled according to salon standards and my outfit was just right. I sashayed my way right to his desk! However, I noticed he was on a call. So, I stood pretty and waited. I just knew he could smell my perfume [that was enough to get his attention]. He wrapped up his call quickly.

After he ended his call, we picked up where we left off. I then headed back to my desk [he was watching me walk]. His coworker, who is a great friend to us now, asked Glover, "Is that your wife?" At the time, we didn't know we'd be each other's forever, but the Holy Spirit prophesied through our friend!

Several weeks later, I was transferred to another department in a different building so we could no longer have our afternoon pop up visits. Glover looked up my new location on our company's intranet and called me on my new office line. He was his usual jovial self. He asked if he could have my cell number and I happily obliged. From there, he randomly called me about once a month for a year. I allowed him to pursue me because I refused to chase a man!

To be honest, I wasn't sure if he would really want anything to do with me once he found out about my *illness*. I didn't want him to think I was crazy. When my girlfriends asked if I was talking to anyone or had any prospects, I referred to Glover as my "gentleman caller".

Finally, the Saturday after Thanksgiving 2006, he called me on his way back from visiting his family in Lakeland, FL. We had our usual, upbeat, fun conversation, when I interrupted him and asked, "So when is this interview process over?" He laughed and was taken aback by my outspokenness. I wanted to know what his intentions were. He asked, "Would you like to go catch a movie and dinner tomorrow afternoon?" I said, "I was wondering when you'd ask...I would love to!"

We began dating. He would call me every evening once he left work. I could almost set my watch to the timing of his calls. His consistency was everything to me. We downloaded with each other the day's happenings and decided when our next outing would be.

One day, after losing my job, I went to visit him. Glover could tell I was very upset. He invited me into his home and set a soothing ambiance. Glover turned off the television and all of the lights. Then we sat on the couch. He said, "Talk to me, you have my undivided attention." For someone whose mind was racing full of ideas and thoughts, that was exactly what I needed. He calmed me down and ensured that I was heard. Undoubtedly, at that moment, I knew he would be a part of my future.

We dated for almost five years before we got engaged. We experienced all types of highs and lows together. We spent every weekend together and planned our future. I encouraged him to become a first-time home buyer and we went on romantic getaways. While I was looking for another job, he made sure that I was covered under his health insurance so that I never was without my psychotropic medications. He also stood with me and my family in fervent prayer, as we grieved the ultimate fatal illness of my baby sister. Anything I thought I needed or desired, he did.

Glover continues to do everything within his power to protect and provide. He is MY KING!

We got engaged on March 19, 2010. Before Glover asked me to marry him, my daddy's pre-approval was mandatory. He is a true southern gentleman. Glover called my parent's home on his way home from work and asked my father if he could stop by for a visit. Daddy said, "Sure, come on over." Glover rang the doorbell. My daddy answered, as he was home alone. Glover followed him into the family room. Daddy sat in his favorite, chocolate-colored leather chair. Glover sat across from him on the sofa. He excitedly said, "I wanted to come over to ask you for Jessica's hand in marriage." Daddy responded right away. "I don't have no problem with that." Glover said, "Thank you." Then he shook daddy's hand and daddy walked my soon-to-be husband to the door.

Glover then came in from what I thought was the office. I came downstairs. He gave me an unusually long hug. He then asked if I was thirsty. I went into the fridge to grab some juice and next to it was a ring box. I was THRILLED! When I turned around, he was on one knee. He called my whole entire name [Jessica Denean Johnson] and popped the question that I anxiously longed to hear, "Would you be my wife?" And of course, I said YES!

After our engagement, during the Christmas holiday, we were shopping at the St. Johns Town Center (in Jacksonville). We were leaving a furniture store headed to Target. As we strolled down the sidewalk, my former-crush and his brother walked out of another store. We literally walked right into them. He called my name and smiled. I greeted him; it was quite awkward. There I was, standing with my past love and my forever future. My ex-crush said, "You better hug me like you know me, girl." So, I gave him a church hug, trying to rush this awkwardness along." We said our goodbyes and walked away. As we were walking, I asked Glover, "Was that weird for you?" He said confidently, "No, it was like I am the heavyweight champion of the world, and when he hugged you, he just held my belt for a minute."

It is amazing how God showed me what I thought was my future, although not bad, he was not my destiny.

Chapter 5

A Spring Wedding

March 19, 2011, I became Mrs. Jessica D. Glover. We tied the knot at The Church of Jacksonville on the city's southside. Our Pastors Michael and Connie Smith performed the ceremony. It was a beautiful, sunny spring day. We had about 200 guests in attendance. I wore a taffeta, off the shoulder white dress, a diamond pendant, a white fascinator, and navy-blue shoes with jewels; blue is my favorite color. My *something borrowed* was one of daddy's handkerchiefs. I held it in my hand along with my white rose bouquet.

Glover looked especially handsome that day. He wore a black tuxedo, white vest, and white tie. We had a cake pop and punch reception. Our special day was holy spirit-filled and more than we ever imagined.

After the wedding, we started planning our perfect little family (baby names and all). We weren't in a rush to start a family, but it was on the horizon, or so we thought. I went to the doctor for my annual checkup. I asked her what I would need to do in order to begin preparing for pregnancy. She shared with me that since I was taking psychotropic medications, I would have to consider coming off my medicine to protect the unborn child during my pregnancy. After much thought and prayer, I decided to do just that. For several months I was OK... I felt fine. My mood was stable, I was even-tempered, I thought I was ready to begin trying to have a baby.

In June of 2012, a few months after our first-year wedding anniversary, things began to change. My mind was high and constantly racing; I could barely sleep. I was easily agitated and was talking to others for long periods of time. My husband began noticing the difference, but he wasn't quite sure what was going on, because he had never witnessed a bipolar manic episode. I began to pick arguments with him for what seemed like no reason. He, as always, was patient with me. I wasn't even aware as to what was happening because my first mental breakdown was almost 10 years earlier.

Chapter 6

Lost in Lala Land… Found in Tampa

In August 2012, I had a training class for my job in Tampa, Florida for one week. I had an argument with Glover. I started packing Saturday night. However, due to my mindset, I packed as if I was leaving indefinitely. I had three suitcases, a fan, snacks, and all types of other mementos. I left on a Sunday afternoon heading to Tampa driving alone, but a part of me felt like I may or may not come back.

I arrived in Tampa, late Sunday night. My mind was still racing. I couldn't sleep. A part of me was excited about the training class, the other part was still upset with Glover. Since Glover and I began dating, we talked every single day unless it was humanly impossible. I remember not calling him very much while I was in training. That was a huge sign that something wasn't right.

In training, I made some new coworker friends. I was learning as much as I could remember, but I started having visions of grandeur. I would see ordinary signs and billboards, but I thought that they were speaking directly to me. I imagined that they were telling me to do things. For example, if I saw a Nike sign that said, "Just Do It", whatever I was thinking at the time I saw the sign, I would go do it. Because of these thoughts, my behavior that week in training was erratic. The instructors began noticing it. I would leave and go to the bathroom for long periods of time. I started singing gospel songs in the bathroom. I had a full worship experience in the bathroom stall as tears streamed down my face.

On the last day of training, the trainer and the senior vice president called me into the conference room. They said that they weren't sure what was going on with me, but they needed to let me know that I couldn't continue in my role because I had missed most of the training. I wept uncontrollably. I tried to give an explanation, but it was unintelligible. They both asked that I gather my things and leave the training location. My mind raced... I was exhausted because I didn't sleep all week. I went back to the hotel that I was staying at, and although I checked out earlier that morning, the staff allowed me to take a nap before they cleaned my room. When I woke up from my nap, my mind snapped.

I got in my car to drive back to Jacksonville, once I got behind the wheel, my mind began to focus on the license plates of moving cars. If the license plate ended with the number five, seven, or eight; I continued to follow them. If it ended with the number six, I stopped following that particular car until I found another car that had the five, seven or eight. I have always been intrigued with the biblical correlation of numbers—that's when I snapped!

It was like a rollercoaster ride. I had no idea where I was going. I started in Tampa, went to Clearwater, and came back to Tampa. It started getting later in the evening on that Friday. I saw a Chick-Fil-A. I went to the drive through and got some dinner. I was still very tired. I still had no clue as to where I was, and I didn't want to go back to Jacksonville. I called Glover and told him that I was heading home, but because I had lost my mind, I simply told him what he expected to hear.

Then I spotted a bowling alley. I took my chocolate-colored Tommy Hilfiger suitcase inside with me. I changed from my business attire into a comfortable t-shirt, a long skirt, sandals, and a straw hat. I went back to my car, and I took off my wedding ring and placed it inside my purse. I made sure my wallet, cell phone, and keys were back inside the car and locked the doors. My mind was beyond discombobulated... "The Jessica I knew wasn't present in sanity." I strutted down the street, rolling my suitcase behind me, looking fabulous yet frantic in my straw hat!

A Filipino man rolled up next to me and asked me if I needed a ride. I fearlessly replied, "Sure. I need a ride to the Salvation Army." He began flirting with me, and I was emphatic,

"Just take me to the Salvation Army or I will jump out of this car!" I think I scared him. He dropped me off in downtown Tampa at the Salvation Army, around 7 p.m.

I rang the doorbell at the Salvation Army and asked if I could come in. One of the staff members came to the door and asked me my name. I told her my name was Jennifer Freeman. For some reason, when people meet me, they mistakenly call me Jennifer instead of Jessica. So, when my mind went to an altered state, I referred to myself as Jennifer. Freeman was the last name of one of the trainers who tried to console me.

A short white lady asked how she could assist me, as I peered through the door. I told her I needed a place to sleep for the night. She asked me for my ID. I began looking for it but didn't realize I left it in my purse (locked inside my car) back at the bowling alley. She could tell that I wasn't fully sane. Ms. "Helpful" told me they didn't have any more beds and that I couldn't stay there. I became hysterically upset and yelled at her. The security guard escorted me to the stairwell to exit the premises. However, I decided I'd sleep there in the stairwell; 15 minutes lapsed before they made me vacate the building completely. The security guard directed me across the street to a homeless shelter called Metropolitan Ministries.

It was dusk, and there was a long line of people waiting to enter the shelter. Although I had never been homeless a day in my life, my mind instantly adjusted. I got in line as if this was a usual practice. People were there from all walks of life. Women with school-aged children, single men, and other mentally challenged people. We all stood in line hoping for a place to lay our heads. When I got to the front of the line, the staff asked for my ID. And just like at the Salvation Army because I didn't have an identification, I was told that I couldn't stay there.

The representative informed me that the Department of Motor Vehicles was open the next day; I said OK and left. My sanity was on a trip to *Never-Never Land.* I was so mentally removed from reality that I could not even feel hunger. Night fell and I went across the street to an open field. This is where the shelter rejects gathered and slept nightly. I leaned over onto my suitcase and attempted to rest. I couldn't rest completely because I was mentally exasperated, and I was fully aware of my surroundings...cars and multiple strangers passed by. I held on to my suitcase for dear life. It was all that I had, and it contained enough evidence to prove I had ascribed to a mistaken identity.

It was early Saturday morning. By this time Glover was worried because I hadn't returned any of his calls and the training ended more than a day ago. He called my parents and informed them about the situation. So, my parent's called Jacksonville authorities and attempted to file a missing person's report. However, the police told them that I wasn't gone long enough to file a report.

Glover arrived at my parent's home around 4:30 a.m. Saturday to devise a plan to find me. He said the only thing he remembers when pulling up to my parent's, was the scene of flashing police lights as he drove up to the house.

Waiting another 24 hours wasn't even an option; Glover and my parents headed to Tampa to find me themselves.

When they arrived, they looked for me at the bus station, several hospitals, the Salvation Army, and their last stop was the Metropolitan Ministries' Homeless Shelter. Miraculously, I was seated inside trying to get a bed for Saturday night. I watched them park their car. Then my parent's got out of the car while Glover remained in the back seat. They asked the staff if anyone had seen Jessica Glover. The staff told them no they had not. My mind was so gone because, again, I provided the fictitious name of Jennifer Freeman. I hid from my parents and Glover; I was ready to start a new life. They searched a few other places then drove back to Jacksonville.

In an attempt to get my license, I walked what seemed like forever to the DMV, and by the time I got there, it was closed. I had no sense of time. I walked back to the shelter and ran into a Jamaican man. He asked, "What are you doing here?" I told him that I was angry with my husband, and I am trying to get my ID so I could stay at the homeless shelter. He told me that he just dropped off his girlfriend at the homeless shelter. He said, "You don't look like you belong here. Do you want to go back to my house, so I can help you reach your husband?" Although my mind was in an altered state, my spiritual sense was very high. I agreed. I was relieved and scared at the same time. I got into his truck, and we left the shelter.

Before we went back to his place, we stopped at the local grocery store. He asked me what I wanted for dinner. I told him that I loved jerk chicken. By this time, I was hungry and realized that I hadn't eaten anything since my last meal at Chick-fil-A. He bought chicken, cabbage, rice, and peas. We went to his home, and he prepared a home cooked meal —It was delicious! I went to the bathroom, because I hadn't used the restroom since Friday at the Salvation Army. My entire body was in an altered state. I felt safe. He told me that his wife was going to come over to help me find my husband— That's right... He had a whole wife who did not live with him, and a homeless girlfriend he'd drop off at the shelter...Then there was me, another homeless and insane stranger living with him. This is why I never question the sovereignty of God; He has a valuable purpose for everyone!

I was in Lala Land… So, I mentally fixated on my former crush. I totally dismissed my feelings [in my mind] for my husband. It was like 12-year-old Jessica surfaced and every thought I had focused on *him*. Thankfully, the stranger who helped me [the Jamaican man] was an angel here on earth.

When the Jamaican man's wife came over, she began to ask me my husband's name and I told her the name of my former crush. She searched for him in Atlanta. Luckily, she didn't find anything. Then she asked if I remembered any phone numbers. The only number I could remember was my parent's home phone number. By that time, Glover and my parents were frantically looking for me. We called them. They were so relieved. I told them that I was OK, but I wasn't ready to come home yet, and I would call back once I was ready.

The Jamaican man, his wife, and his girlfriend, all made me feel right at home. I ate delicious authentic Jamaican food, slept on a pullout sofa bed, and although my mind constantly raced, I felt safe. I concluded that my marriage was over, and I was going to find my former crush and live happily ever after.

Glover blew the Jamaican man's phone up! I finally spoke with him and gave him the address to where I was located. Glover and my parents came from Jacksonville for the second time in two days. Once they arrived, Glover immediately came through the door and shook the Jamaican man's hand. He handed him some money for taking care of me. I had so many emotions. I was happy to see everyone, but I was still angry with Glover...I asked him if we could go into the bathroom so we could talk privately. I looked Glover in his eyes and told him that I no longer wanted to be married.

Indignantly, I confessed, "I'm moving back to Atlanta to find my former crush." I really couldn't tell what he was thinking; however, he was definitely shocked and worried, but he kept a calm demeanor. I could tell he agreed with me just to have me stop talking. Then we walked out of the bathroom. That was the first time he witnessed—with his own eyes— me out of my mind. This was one of those for better or for worse challenges.

I was able to remember the name of the bowling alley, so they found the address and my car. I was famished, so we stopped at McDonalds. I scarfed down a Filet-O-Fish Meal. Glover drove me back to Jacksonville in our car as my parents followed. My mind was in Lala Land, I was still angry with Glover, and I desperately wanted to find my former crush.

Chapter 7

Two Months... Two Psych Ward Stays

Once we arrived back in Jacksonville, I didn't want to stay at our home with Glover. I decided to spend the night with my parents. My mom helped me shower and tried to put me to bed. I was still quite delusional. I was afraid to sleep alone. She put both twin beds in my sister's childhood room together and we rested. I didn't want my mom to leave my side.

The next morning, my mother and Glover took me to my primary care physician for an evaluation. By this time, I had slightly calmed down. However, I knew I was safe because I was with my family. It was like a sense of peace came over me, even though my heart knew this was just the beginning of finding a solution to my insanity.

I was taken to Memorial Hospital's Psychiatric Ward. This is the hospital where I was born. Thirty-five years later, I was back, fighting for my sanity. While in the holding room, waiting to be admitted, Glover and my mom waited with me. I couldn't stop talking about my former crush. My mind was stuck in a false sense of a romantic Lala Land.

Compassionately, my mother explained to Glover that he was my first crush. A nurse came in to ask me questions about my mental state. She asked me if I had suicidal thoughts, although I didn't, I said *yes*. Glover wept uncontrollably. The reality of my insanity finally hit him. Then I was admitted— no straight jacket necessary.

I was placed on a co-ed ward. It was very similar to my first experience back in Atlanta… zombie-like patients that were heavily medicated walking the halls. We received psychiatric visits from doctors, different medications, planned activities, and three meals a day. This was Glover's initiation to another part of my world.

He, my parents, and other village members, visited religiously. Every Tuesday and Thursday at 7:30 p.m. someone would come sit with me. Some days I was happy to see them, other days, not so much. My emotions toward Glover were equally bipolar. My mind and body attempted to adjust to the various medications. The doctors worked tirelessly to develop an individualized treatment plan that would work best for me.

After about two weeks, I started to feel better. Various components of my sanity reappeared a little bit each day. I was no longer thinking of my former-crush; however, I wasn't sure I wanted to be married anymore. I was getting better, but I wasn't 100 percent.

I met some new friends. For some reason, my love for the hair industry was magnified during this time of mental instability. I became fixated on becoming a hairstylist. I styled various patients' hair every morning. I used hospital body lotion as styling lotion and created cornrows. They met me in the common area to get their hair done before breakfast.

I asked Glover to write down my friends' cell phone numbers. We could not have cell phones in the ward, but we could utilize the community phone. I called a few friends; although, I still wasn't in my right mind, they were all gracious. I was trying to relocate because I didn't want to stay in Jacksonville anymore.

I had one friend come on visitation days a few times. She brought me socks, lip gloss, and notebooks to journal my feelings. She proved her loyalty to our friendship during one of my lowest moments. Honestly, most people fear or don't know how to process their feelings towards those battling mental illness, so they distance themselves. I am eternally grateful to those who stayed.

My time at Memorial eventually came to an end. I operated at about a 40 percent sanity level. I still had some erratic behavior, but I functioned a little better. It felt so good to be outside and feel the fall breeze on my face. I was confined in the psychiatric ward for about a month, but it seemed like forever. I was under the impression that I was finally going home, but Glover and my parents had already arranged my admission to another mental health facility. They wanted to ensure I wasn't being prematurely released. I didn't care... I was furious! I wanted to start working on my transition plan to leave Jacksonville. Who were they to stop my fantasies of grandeur!?!

Psych Ward #2

My mom took me to her house to take a shower, change clothes, and to gather some personal items. Then she drove me to the other psychiatric hospital. I grabbed my luggage and refused to let her help me. I admitted myself to Wekiva Springs Hospital. I informed the staff that I didn't want *any* visitors.

Once admitted, I was taken to the women's wing. This was an extremely different experience. It was like a big slumber party. Cliques of women partnered off together dressed in pajamas and sweats. Some groups were giving each other pedicures and manicures, some looking through magazines together, some watching movies, and others making arts and crafts. However, I was ready to GO... I felt out of place!

My appearance and attire have always been important to me. I dressed myself in black slacks, a silk dressy blouse, classy flats, and jewelry. I was still upset that I was even there. I just decided to sit on the edge of one of the couches to take in the environment.

One of the nurses approached me and started asking me about another patient. I told her that I was a patient. She apologized; she had mistaken me for another therapist. I have to say, I was a little proud. It made me see that despite my location, I wasn't destined to be in a state of mental instability forever. At minimum, I didn't LOOK crazy.

I stayed there for about three weeks. This time was different though. I was all alone. Unlike at Memorial, there, I knew that every Tuesday and Thursday, someone was coming to visit me. This gave me time to think and pray. I journaled, made arts and crafts, and devised a transition plan.

I met an older African-American woman who reminded me of my paternal grandmother. I was immediately drawn to her. She was wheelchair bound. We would talk for hours. Because my mind wasn't 100 percent yet, I imagined that I was speaking with my grandmother. I took it as my duty to make sure she was OK. I would roll her into the cafeteria for meals, make sure she had something to drink, I even gave her a pedicure. She gave me a sense of community and purpose while I was there.

I still had a list of phone numbers of my friends. I called my college girlfriend in Atlanta. We both majored in psychology, and she was studying to become a licensed therapist. Her understanding of the mind and its fragility was a true gift to me. I was paranoid that someone was listening in on my conversation, so I whispered while I spoke with her. I began telling her my plans to leave Glover. She listened to me with no judgement and tried to console me. She let me continue to share my plan. I was determined to begin my new life in the place I became an adult– Atlanta.

During this stay, the doctors were still trying to discover the right medication for me. I think at the end of my stay at Wekiva Springs Hospital, I was at about 60 percent sane. I reached out to my social worker and told her I was ready to leave.

The next day, I packed my bags and waited for the shuttle service to arrive. I told the driver to take me to parent's home. When I arrived, my parents were surprised, because for about three weeks, I had not spoken to anyone outside of the hospital. I'm sure they didn't know what to expect.

This time, things were a little better; however, I still had it in my head that I was leaving Glover. I called a good friend of mine who is like a brother to me. I asked him to pick me up and take me home. He reluctantly agreed. My brother knew something wasn't right, but he drove me anyway.

When I arrived unannounced, I opened the front door, turned off the alarm, and went upstairs to clean out my closet. Glover was very upset! He kept trying to get me to talk to him, I wouldn't say a word. My mind was fixated on leaving. Glover asked my friend to leave, and he obliged.

Once I packed my bags, I told Glover to take me back to my parent's home. Glover then called my sister in Colorado to talk to me. I remember telling her that she can handle her marriage and I would handle mine. I was very angry and belligerent. Glover had given me no reason to be angry, it was just my unstable, not properly medicated mind making me think Glover had done something wrong, and it was time to leave.

Glover took me to my parent's home. I gathered my things from his car, and I told him that I would be moving in with my parents in preparation to relocate to Atlanta. He just stood there and listened. He realized that it wasn't his wife, but the illness speaking on my behalf.

Chapter 8

Restored Marriage...with Children?

When I told Glover I was leaving him, he, understandably so, was very short with me. He tried to listen to me but didn't invest any emotions. During this time, he was never quite sure who he was speaking with. One moment, I was lucid and stable and the next, I was unbalanced and making outlandish statements. He didn't know what to do or who to call.

One Saturday evening, while staying at my parent's, I called Glover and asked if he could come and pick me up for church on Sunday. He reluctantly agreed. Sunday morning, I woke up early and began my routine of hair, makeup, and getting dressed. I wanted to make sure that I was extra cute especially because Glover hadn't seen me in a few weeks.

After I finished getting dressed, I opened my bible and began to read. It was the first time I read the bible in weeks without thoughts of grandeur. I was truly grasping the concepts in which I read. I read the scripture, John 10:10, *The thief cometh not, but that he may steal, and kill, and destroy; I came that they may have life and may have it abundantly.* As soon as I read it my mind snapped back to 100 percent sanity! In that moment, I realized this whole ordeal was designed to kill, steal, and destroy the blessings God placed on my life and my marriage. Team Glover would not be dismantled, and I was determined to fight for my marriage.

When Glover arrived to pick me up for church, I greeted him at the door, grabbed both of his hands, looked him in his eyes and apologized for all that I had put him through. The look in his eyes was one of relief. He recognized me [his sane wife was back]. He knew that I was in my right mind, speaking to him from a place of love and sanity. On our ride to church, we talked like we did prior to this ordeal…an upbeat, jovial, and fun conversation. We grabbed a bite to eat for breakfast and headed to church.

Praise and worship that Sunday was like none we ever experienced because we were giving thanks for my sanity. We made it through the hardest storm we had ever faced. I will never forget it. The choir sang a song that Sunday called "Thank You Lord" by Walter Hawkins. The lyrics comforted me…

Tragedies are commonplace

All kinds of diseases, people are slipping away

Economies down, people can't get enough pay

As for me all I can say is

Thank you, Lord, for all you've done for me

Yeah, yeah, yeah

Folks without homes

Living out in the streets and the drug habit some say

They just can't beat

Muggers and robbers, no place seems to be safe

But You've been my protection every step of the way

I wanna say, thank you Lord for all You've done for me

Yeah, yeah

It could have been me (thank you)

Outdoors (thank you)

No food (thank you)

No clothes (thank you)

Or left alone (thank you)

Without a friend (thank you)

Or just another number (thank you)

With a tragic end (thank you)

But you didn't see fit (thank you)

To let none of these things be (thank you)

'Cause everyday by your power (thank you)

You keep on keeping me (thank you)

And I wanna say

(Thank you) for all you've done for me

I wanna say (Thank you lord for all you've done for me.

I lost it (but in a good way)! I cried uncontrollably in praise during that song. I reflected on the fact that I was in another city, out of my mind, sleeping in a field, taken in by a stranger, yet God protected me. Anything could have happened to me, but like the previously referenced song, *"He didn't see fit, to let none of these things be!"*

After church, Glover and I went back to our home and reconnected. I asked him to put my wedding ring back on my ring finger. He happily agreed. The joy in his eyes to finally connect and share with me what transpired during the past three months was intimately amazing.

However, we decided that I'd stay with my parents until we received counseling from our church. That was difficult because I longed to be at home with him. But for the first time in months, I had something to look forward to. Glover wanted to make sure that I wasn't on another roller coaster ride in my mind and that this was real. Once we completed counseling, I moved back home.

Being back at home was great. Glover and I loved being together again. Even though we were happy, and I was fully sane,

I was still adjusting to my medication. The medicine made me lethargic. I rested most days and got out of bed to take a shower about an hour before Glover came home from work each day. My psychiatrist was God-sent! He worked with me for several months until we found the right medication. Dr. Shah has since retired, but to this day, my family and I still call his name in prayer.

Every day, I called my girlfriend and we talked for hours. She was dealing with health complications. We chatted about our hopes, dreams, and our hard-working husbands. We were both extremely grateful for our wonderful men of God.

Glover told me that he would take care of all of the bills, and I didn't have to worry about anything. While I was in the hospital, he started an application for me with Social Security to secure my disability benefits. He said that all of the benefit checks would be mine to do whatever I wanted; I hesitantly agreed.

I called Social Security to discuss my application. I spoke with an African American woman. She reviewed my paperwork, asked me several questions about my education and various jobs I had. She saw that I held an insurance license, and that I was a former Series 7 and Series 63 licensed stockbroker. She very directly said, "Ma'am, with your background, education, and previous job history, I will not approve you for your social security disability benefits. You can definitely find a way to provide for yourself. Your application is DENIED."

I was offended and relieved at the same time. However, her words confirmed, again, that I was far from crazy. Nevertheless, I wanted more, I just did not have any idea how to obtain it.

For years, I looked for jobs, with no success. I attempted some entrepreneurial endeavors as well. I wanted to find a sense of purpose, but it seemed like nothing worked.

I finally landed a job with a national insurance company in their call center working part time. It was a great reintroduction into the workforce. The pay was low, but that wasn't my focus… getting back on a daily schedule was. I found my rhythm again—I felt so accomplished!

I was a team leader, awarded prizes and recognized as a great employee. My confidence skyrocketed. After going through my mental breakdown, this job showed me that with time and effort, anything was possible. I didn't lose my ability to learn and work successfully.

One Saturday afternoon while working at the call center, I was speaking to a client and all of a sudden, I blacked out. I had a seizure at my desk. Glover was called and immediately came to take me to the emergency room. I was hospitalized for a few days and told that I could not drive for a year.

During this sobering moment of dealing with Bipolar Disorder— coupled with seizures— we decided parenthood was not an option for us… We would be Team Glover, a party of two for life. I did not want Glover to take on the responsibility of children if something were to happen to me mentally or physically. We decided to live in a perpetual honeymoon state forever! Our vision is to build a legacy for our nieces, nephews, and God-children.

Chapter 9

Success In Sanity

It has been 10 years since my last mental health breakdown. My prayer is that it was my last. My husband and I work daily to create an environment that is peaceful, full of love and joy. We make sure that my schedule is not packed and that I have time to rest if needed. Dr. Shah found the correct medications for my Bipolar Disorder and seizures. Since then, my mental and physical health have been sustained.

Every day, I have a routine surrounding taking my medicine. I realized taking it at night works best for me. It calms my mind and stops the racing thoughts. This allows me to rest peacefully. Therefore, at 7:30 p.m., after dinner— while watching Judge Judy— I take my medicine.

Consistently taking my prescribed medications has changed my life. When I decided in 2012 to stop taking my medicine, it opened the door to temporary insanity. I almost walked away from my marriage because my mind allowed me to believe that something was wrong when everything was right.

Mental illness is sneaky. One moment, you are fine, the next you are unstable and erratic. What I have found is that treating it every day, even when you are at your best, is the remedy. The medication ensures your brain receives the chemicals needed to function properly. Mental illness is a chemical imbalance. However, we as a community must view it like any other illness. People who suffer from diabetes take medication like insulin to balance their blood sugar—mental illness is no different.

Far too often, people with mental illness self-medicate. Marijuana and other drugs, alcohol, and sex are often used to numb the pain of mental illness or to stimulate a temporary high. These "solutions" often lead to other issues of addiction. Consulting with a medical professional to determine the right treatment is key to living a productive life despite being mentally ill. Since consistently taking my medication daily, God has allowed so many opportunities to come into my life... Let's call it, *Success in Sanity*.

I have been a thriving licensed realtor for the last four years. I have sold millions of dollars in real estate throughout Florida and Georgia. I interact with clients, brokers, and other vendors daily to make dreams of homeownership come true. The rewarding feeling of helping others and providing for my family is a naturally sane high!

I also found, with the help of my therapist, that I would be a great recruiter. So, in the spring of 2021, I landed a contractor role as a corporate recruiter for a national healthcare company. Every day, I make job offers to others. I get to experience the sheer joy and excitement of candidates all over the nation accepting my offers for employment…another naturally sane high. This role provides consistency and a flexible schedule. Recruiting coupled with real estate sales have proven to be just right for me.

My husband and I just celebrated our 11th year of marriage. Our love for each other continues to grow and evolve. Glover truly honored the vows he made, to be with me in sickness and in health… for THIS I am eternally grateful. This year, we were able to reach our own personal real estate goal. We just completed building a waterfront home perfect for the two of us. TO GOD BE THE GLORY!

The goal in sharing these successes is to demonstrate that having a mental illness is not a death sentence or a sentence to live a mediocre life. Working with medical professionals to find the right medication, will allow you the ability to live a productive life.

The term success is relative. What is successful to me, may not be success for someone else. We all have the privilege of deciding what success means. Taking medication, lying in bed all day, and taking a shower one hour before my husband came home was not the life I wanted to live. Seeking the help of a therapist and re-entering the workforce helped me realize I was more than capable of achieving any goal I set.

Chapter 10

Far From Crazy...

I'm far from crazy and I'm closer to fulfilling my divine purpose than I've ever been. However, walking my sanity out has never been easy, but I've developed a plan that works. I've also accepted the fact that I have a mental illness. More importantly, I am unashamed! While my father may have never said these words: "I have a mental illness," I can, and I do. This fact alone makes me proud. Yes, I have a mental illness, but *mental illness* doesn't have me– I'm completely sane.

Do I ever see myself coming off my medication? Absolutely *not*, because I desire to remain sane, and successful throughout my life. Thus, I have adopted this mantra: "Accept. Medicate. Thrive. REPEAT."

Accept

We each have unique personalities, physical differences, and mental capabilities. God created each person according to His purpose. So often, I have heard people tell me, *"Jessica, don't say you have a mental illness. You are owning something that God didn't want to be yours."* I absolutely disagree. I don't believe God gave me this illness, but I know that he has provided the remedy to live a full life. God positioned doctors, therapy, and the exact medication to help balance my brain. This is how I maintain my sanity.

Far too often people living with mental illnesses don't want to accept that they are, indeed, sick. We have to take ownership of our reality. Praying it away is not the only solution. Our brains need to be chemically balanced with the proper treatment. Unfortunately, family members and friends get frustrated with loved ones battling mental illnesses because they refuse help. There can be no permanent solution without acceptance.

Medicate

Medication for a lifetime is another reality we must accept. It was the *angel* nurse at the first psych ward who enlightened me about how to view my medication. She said, "Medicine is a form of healing!" Not only were her words revelatory, but they changed my life, forever.

Changing our perspective regarding psychotropic medication is vital because without it, you will end up crazy. At the onset of accepting my mental illness, I resented taking medication. I asked, *"why do I have to take this every day?"* So, purposely I skipped a day or two. This gave me what I thought was a sense of control of my sanity. I thought, let me take it when I want to take it. I quickly learned that randomly taking the medicine did not give my brain what it needed. I understood I needed medication, daily, to thrive.

Therefore, every day I take my medicine, I wake up refreshed and ready to handle marriage, business, and life. Mental illness doesn't mean you cannot lead a normal, healthy, and successful life, I'm living proof that you can.

When I was declared indigent there was help for me (without health insurance). For those who are uninsured, www.goodrx.com is a tremendous resource. On this website you will find lists of various medications that are discounted. It also has charts showing you which pharmacy has the lowest price for each medication. It is my sincerest prayer and hope that our government will provide additional support services for those without health insurance who battle mental illness.

Thrive

Although I live with mental illness, which is genetic; success is also in my DNA. Consequently, I decided to *thrive because I possessed* a burning desire to grow past the stigma of *"Girl, she's crazy!"* When I realized I was watching television all day, I had to come to grips with the fact that I needed to be productive; I longed for more. I had to advocate for myself and seek an individualized treatment plan that worked for me.

Once the medication was right, I had more energy. Then I was able to re-enter the workforce as a stable part-time employee. However, when I mastered that, I still yearned for more; so, I became relentless. In 2018, I achieved my ultimate career goal of becoming a licensed realtor.

Giant steps weren't necessary for my success… but God-ordered steps were! I took those steps one at a time to achieve my personal goals. My success didn't happen overnight, but each day of my life is an opportunity for me to better myself (you can too). Don't allow mental illness to rob you of an *insanely* successful life. Thriving in every area of life is the essence of success. Find what works for you!

REPEAT

NEVER give up, establish a circle of support that understands you, and ALWAYS be willing to start over when necessary. I learned to ask for what I wanted, and I stopped settling for what was handed to me. This includes how I saw mental illness through others and myself. I faced myself completely, and asked, "Is this all you want?"

Each day I am intentional about reaching my goals. I have a strong support system that doesn't allow me to sulk in my illness. Everyone around me is winning because my tribe is goal-oriented. It's true we become who we surround ourselves with.

So, if you desire to be successful in sanity, evaluate where you are, and who is in that place with you.

My therapist taught me not to cut others off, but to reposition them. When we find that relationships are no longer mutually beneficial, we must prioritize them appropriately.

Individuals facing mental illness, aren't society's *crazy rejects*. We each have a voice; we each have a purpose and we all have a divine calling on our lives. Usually, the secret truths about who we are, are the very things that need to be confessed, exposed, and properly dealt with. *Unashamed* is the mentality I have wholly embraced. I am *Far From Crazy…* because I accepted my truth, and it has catapulted me to my *Success in Sanity*!

About the Author

Jessica Johnson Glover is a prolific, speaker, passionate mental health advocate, and realtor. She earned a Bachelor's degree in psychology from Clark Atlanta University.

After 20 years of living successfully with a mental illness, Jessica realized she possessed the skills and knowledge to help people who silently suffer from mental illnesses. Purposely, Jessica established and founded *The Success In Sanity Society (SISS)*, an accountability tribe for those who are unashamed and ready to successfully maintain their sanity. In this community, Jessica conducts monthly virtual meetings that help individuals successfully manage mental illness and live the life of their dreams.

Her story of tragedy turned triumph proves that anyone suffering with a mental illness can be successful. Jessica's proven formula for success involves four simple steps: Accept, Medicate, Thrive, Repeat!

Jessica is married to her soulmate, Gerald L. Glover, a mortgage professional. They reside in sunny Jacksonville, Florida.

Her moments of purposeful self-care include spending time with her family and friends, listening to gospel music, getting pampered, and binge watching some of her favorite television shows with her husband.

Invitation to Success In Sanity Society

If you've been enlightened by this literary experience, I would love to offer continued support, inspiration, and empowerment for your journey!

You're NOT alone!

I am certain no one simply 'gets over' THIS! It is a lifetime work, and we must create and implement routines for continual success.

Systems of support are vital.

Within the Success In Sanity Society (S.I.S.S.) you will connect with myself and other women who are courageously taking this journey too. This is the ideal space for YOU!

For more details on how to join, go to:

www.SuccessInSanity.com

CPSIA information can be obtained
at www.ICGtesting.com
Printed in the USA
BVHW030440160722
641986BV00009B/270